MW00490507

FINDING ME

GIANNA SHAMONE

These written words are dedicated
to my two mums.

One, wrote my favourite collection of children's
stories and inspired me to write as a child.
The other encourged me to write and
publish in my adulthood.

Together, you form my foundation.
I love you.

In order to overcome the pain and the confusion and transform into a new me, my inner being began to bring meaning to the feelings inside of me and birthed them into these poems.

May they accompany
your journey.

CONTENT

I AM...

CONFUSED

I lost myself
along the way
and I can't
remember where.

Blur.
Cloudy vision.
No vision.
Nothing.

By day I keep busy.
At night I make up scenarios
how to get you back
- until it's time to be busy again.

I don't want to feel this way no more.
I don't want to want you no more.
I don't want to miss you no more.
I don't want to cry over you no more.
And yet I do.

And I can hear the echoes
of my unspoken words -
wandering in my head.
Fueling the anxieties.
Restless, ruthless, cruel.

I can feel my face looks sad.
Eyes are fixed and glassy.
The smile that rushes over my face
so effortlessly at times
seems so far gone -
it scares me.

Rephrasing every word in my head that
I said to you the last time I saw you.
Trying to find the right words that would have
changed the outcome of you leaving me.

My soul is aching for yours.

I am strong.
I can own this.
I know I can.
But I don't want to.
I want to be weak.
I want to miss you now.
Because this makes me feel closer to you.
Probably the closest I'll ever get to you again.

From disbelief, to shocking realization,
to painful acceptance.
Just to go back to the beginning of disbelief.
The circle has to be walked a couple of times,
until it can be released.

I can see the pain in his eyes –
it seems like the pain of the entire world
decided to rest in them.

I wonder what my future self feels,
I wonder what she's like.
She must be strong and brave and –
happy -
Since she lives past the pain
I find myself drowning in once again;
Numbing me and my potential.

... and just so I would never lose you entirely,
I was saving with my mind -
what was lost with the eye.
Every line formed by laughter.
Every line caused by pain.
Every inch of your body.
is telling me the story of your life.

Sometimes you feel torn apart.
One part wants to flee back
to the one your heart longs for,
but the other is holding you back
because deep down you know
it's time to let go.

I miss summer.
I miss the feeling of the sunbeams on my face.
I miss the feeling that nothing can bring me down -
because of all the extra energy I absorbed
throughout the day.
I miss the person I was last summer.

Every time I'm trying to overwrite my story -
you come creeping up in the back of my head.
So present, so persistent.
Clearly you came to stay for a little longer.
And I can feel my shield weaken and...
I am letting it down one last time.

One last time –
to dwell.
To cry over the ghosts that are left –
from when we were US.

My mind racing. Fast.
Spiraling rather down than up –
Leaving me confused.

Insecurities lurking in all of us –
Waiting for the right opportunity
to come to the surface and fuck with our minds.

I feel blocked;
In so many ways;
On so many levels;
On so many days –
Lately.

I still think of you
sometimes -
When I touch myself.

Venus retrogate.
Everything comes back. Back in a Rush.
Not as dramatic as back then -
But intense enough to keep me up at night.
Wide awake -
walking down memory lane.
Bad memories -
Good memories -
Ones I will treasure -
always.

Feeling lost –
What to do?   Write
Where to go?   Inward
What to feel?   Liberated
Who to be?   Me

I JUST WANT TO BE MY TRUE SELF

BUT I CANT GET MYSELF TO DO IT

Finding words to name the stinging pain,
and releasing it through the flow of my tears.
Until – at some point - the pain gets less terrorizing,
the unanswered questions quiet down
and the tears run less frequently.
It's time to welcome a new circle into my life
– the circle of self-love.
Finding ways of putting the smile back on my face.

... and then she just decided
to be strong again.

Life is funny sometimes.
It hits you with, what you consider as a big loss
at that moment -
and then it turns out to be exactly what you needed -
to get to the next level.
Open your eyes and look out for the signs.

And once again it's this.
This right here that keeps me sane.
Releasing all the confusion in my head
through words on paper.
Giving my all-over-the-place-thoughts
structure and meaning and breathing life into them
and in return they breath life back into me.

I used to run from loneliness,
I used to run from facing my inner self,
my inner voice -
So life forced me to spend time with myself
and it made me shake from crying
like I never cried before.
It made me question life - my life -
it made me loose my mind sometimes...
But loneliness also taught me who I was,
who I am and who I want to be.
I know now, this journey needed to be
and I am so grateful for it.

And all of the sudden they are back.
Undeniably there – wetting my face.
Every single drop of my emotions
resembles something.
I know it - I can feel it.
There is intensity to them, heaviness almost,
making sure I don't ignore them.
Because they are meaningful –
and it frustrates me
that I just can't wrap my head around it.
Patience was never mine to have.

Feel every emotion deeply.
Not only happiness and love,
but grief, madness, confusion ...
Every emotion is a part of you
and needs to be felt -
in order for you to be your true self.

We are in our heads a lot.
We make up reasons why
and stories to certain behaviors
of the beings around us.
Getting lost in a net of eventualities.

We tend to put on a mask every single day -
for our colleagues at work,
for our friends, even for ourselves at times.
Copying what we see
instead of listening inward
and following that inner voice.
Trust me, this voice will not shut up -
it will not go away until you listen.
Take off the mask
and find the strength to be you.

I gave you all the love I had,
I gave you more than I could give
and yet it wasn't enough.
It wasn't what you needed
and so I took it back, back for myself.
I took it back for the sake of my well-being
and peace of mind.
I transformed it into the strongest gift
I could give myself.
Forgiveness –
which turned into self-love and balance.
And till this day I hold this gift
in the depths of my heart.

- s/o to the Queen Sade

She looked up,
tears flowing down like waterfalls.
She prayed to be able to get over him -
every single night.
Without knowing who she was talking to
she hoped for her prayers to be heard.
And all of the sudden she began
to find the answer herself.
- the healing began.

SEEK TRUTH
What is it that I am looking for?
What is it that brings me joy?
What's my purpose?
How can I implement these things into my career?

Just because I can do certain things,
doesn't mean I have to do them.
I am here to be happy and reach my fullest potential.

Questions I've been working on answering -
and epiphanies that came along the way.

After all, you still want my body,
my warmth…
But it's not for you to have no more.

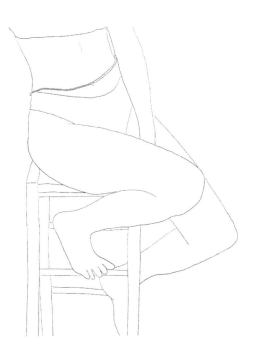

And suddenly there was this moment of truth
yesterday -
the moment I saw him and her.
Him and his new love.
She's a girl more than a woman –
quiet, almost shy, but with a spark of rebellion.
She knew who I was - I felt it.
I saw it in the way she looked at me –
over and over again.
I hope she feels the way I did
when I was with him
before everything started to fall apart.

Sometimes you feel like,
you are standing right next to your body.
As if you are not really connected to yourself.
Everything seems to go by in slowmotion
and you have the feeling of missing everything.
That's your soul aching for alone-time,
reconnection and forgiveness towards yourself.

Sinking -
almost drowning in this ocean of emotions.
Blinded by all these tears -
loosing myself.
Until - I finally see my reflection
right in front of me.
And I'm back.

I haven't seen you in a long time.
At first I thought I needed you
in my life to survive.
I told myself -
even if we can't be together,
at least I need to see you once in a while.
But it's like they say:
"out of sight out of mind" –
at least after a while.
I'm happy I can actually feel this way.

Empty pages.
But slowly my feelings
form words to express themselves -
flowing through my entire body,
my veins, my fingertips -
until I am finally ready to release them
through the pen in my hand.
Leaving a feeling of relief and calmness
where there was confusion and restlessness.

Freeing myself from you
was the best decision
and yet the hardest thing
I ever had to do.

I AM...

HEALING

Rise, rise high my love
and leave the fear behind -
there is no need for it no more.

Smile through it all.
Even if it's a fake smile -
force yourself to smile in front of the mirror.
And after a little while you will come to realize
that it forms itself into a genuine one -
rushing through your entire body
as pure, positive energy.

"I am fierce, I am strong. I am fearless"
She tells her own reflection in the mirror
before she leaves her safe place,
her comfort-zone, her home –
to step outside and conquer the world.

Currently channeling my old self.
More insecurities, more anxieties -
less knowledge about me and life itself.
But eager to learn, practice and eventually
level up.

The endless sea of chances is found
outside the comfort zone of habit.
- Go swim.

No one tasted my juice in a long time.
Drove along the curves of my body
with their finger, or tongue –
or caressed my lips, my breasts, my thighs,
my…

But the juice is still flowing,
my curves are still round,
my hips, my breasts, my thighs are still here,
waiting to be felt.

Like a majestic tree, I can feel my roots.
Strong, solid and anchored
in the essence of my true being.

You are a never-ending puzzle –
with missing pieces.

- Papa

Fear, failure... all the big words
that kept me from even trying.
But in the end,
that is what they are and not more,
just big words.

Words fueled with meaning by people
who are paralyzed by the thought
of what other people might think.
Here is the funny part though,
other people don't really think
that much about you and your life,
because they're figuring out their own shit.

The time is now.
There will be no right timing in the future,
there will be no moment where the fear is gone.
Start now.

You are the one in charge -
use your power.

Waves of assurance and euphoria
washing down my riverbed of emotions,
since I decided to listen to that inner voice.
Fear is a constant companion –
but I feel more and more confident
in following this path despite of it.

Note to myself:
Good morning beautiful,
You are enough -
you are more than enough.
In fact you are awesome!
You are smart, you are pretty,
you are a good person
and you deserve the world.

Life…
the small things
the birds singing
the last free spot in the sun
the random encounters
reading the first page of a new book
waking up with a smile
… is good.

New Beginning.
The need to shift some parts of my life around
became so loud,
that I couldn't ignore it anymore.
And I will now rise out of the ashes of the old me
and embrace the new me -
with acceptance for possible missteps along the way,
to find the best version of myself.

The path I'm taking has obstacles.
And many turning points ahead -
making it impossible to see the end.
But I learned to trust my journey and intuition -
to guide me through all the tough parts -
and my heart - to enjoy the positive ones.
So I take it step by step -
with eager anticipation of what's to come.

What is holding you back
from showing the real you?

I want to know who you are.
I want to know what you feel.
I want to know where you've been.
I want to know what you saw.

- Papa

I'm feeling the shift.
I can feel how my spirit, my soul
and my consciousness are evolving.
I am aware of negative thoughts much faster
and am able to redirect my thinking
to more positive formed beliefs.
I love this evolution of myself
and am grateful to feel safe and mentally stable
to dedicate some time, every day -
to continue this journey.

Do you know that feeling,
when everything just makes sense?
Even the excruciating situation that seemed so random
and just cruel to you when it happened,
fits and makes sense all of the sudden?
These moments are the doorway to change.
Walk through the door.

I'm ready.
Ready to fall in love again.
I'm ready to kiss someone and feel overwhelmed
every time it happens.
I'm ready to be stunned again.
Ready to feel as if no one but that person -
can make me feel this way.
I have so much love to give and I am finally ready
to give it to someone else but you.

August 9th 2019
Today I am following all the ideas
stuck in my head.
Letting them out -
to breath, to grow, to prosper.
Helping me -
breath, grow and prosper.

This juice of mine is pure.
This juice of mine is real.
This juice of mine can cure.
This juice of mine is a 4 course meal.

When you take the time and treat me right,
this juice of mine will flow all night.

I truly believe in the healing powers
of experiencing pain – excruciating pain, even.
It raises questions, which might not have come up
for you before.
It makes you question yourself, your behavior
and reactions towards others, but more importantly,
towards yourself. And this hopefully leads to
changing your perspective and behavior in some
areas. It is a potential turning point and could wake
you up, if you let it.
This then gives you the chance to break your own
unhealthy patterns, which formed themselves
through your upbringing, your lived-through
experiences – good and bad ones -
as well as the vision you created for yourself. To get
to this point of understanding the need to unlearn
certain toxic patterns,
you need to be ready to go through all the emotions -
feel through them, live through them.

Give them space to be, to exist - acknowledge them.
Scream when you are angry and mad, let the surplus
energy out by movement; walk it off, dance it off,
work out– whatever it is that gives you back your
peace of mind. Cry when you are sad, lonely,
confused.
Imagine your feelings are embodied in every single
tear pouring out of your soul and eventually out of
your body.
Let them all go - do it as often
as you feel it's necessary, but don't lose yourself in it.
Use it as a channel, your personal channel of letting
go of hurtful emotions.

You create your transition; you have the power to
mold your own personal way of dealing with your
emotions.

It's your guiding system.
Pay attention.

Have you ever lost the craft
to verbalize your thoughts?

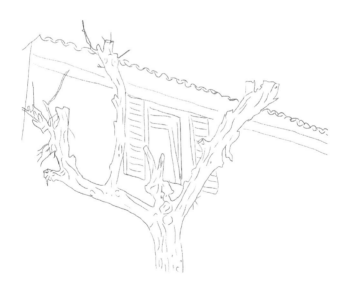

I don't believe in coincidences.
I don't believe that you meet people
without a purpose.
I don't believe in being resentful –
But Frank taught me:
You got to believe in something.
So I believe in love.

- s/o to Frank Ocean

Intimacy has many faces
and doesn't have to be physical.
It can be a deep look into someone else's eyes.
A compassionate gesture.
Listening to someone else's story of pain...

What is the purpose of a plant growing,
if she ends up staying rooted
in the same place?

Don't be afraid of change.
Embrace it.
Enjoy the time in your cocoon -
it is not wasted.
You are healing, growing, evolving.
And when the time has come you'll rise my love,
rise until you reach your highest potential.

Lay your head in the palm of my hand
and let all the emotions run down your face.
I am here to hold you.
I am here to guard you.
I am here to love you.

Let down your walls and show me your innerness.

Always drawn to the light.
Always choosing sun over shadow.
Always experiencing my mood being lifted
after the sun decides to softly kiss my face.
Always feeling liberated and at peace
- with all that lives around me -
when the warmth touches my skin.

Always kinda knew - I'm a child of light.

Sometimes there are obstacles on your way
to the next goal.
Don't let them stop you.
And don't loose faith.
They are there to navigate you.
At times you think you know what's best,
but the universe knows better.

I AM...

GROWING

My consciousness -
unfiltered and raw -
fuses into my writing and visual work.
I swallow what the world gives me.
Day in day out. Scenario after scenario.
And it marinates in my innerness for a bit,
until it is birthed into art.
That's the healing power I created for myself.
Experiencing – sitting with it – taking it in – feeling it.

Feeling it by myself,
in calmness, warmth and comfort.
So I can listen carefully and sense it and
let it guide me.
Towards another piece to read,
feel and heal through.

Break of dawn.
Calm and peaceful.
The only sound cutting the silence
is the language of the birds.
They sing a melody
which is so accurately fitting the scenery
that it almost seems directed and planned.
Helping me to tune into my day.

Feeling what others feel -
because I automatically channel their emotions
with such an overwhelming intensity –
that I mistake them for mine.

Movements -
smooth yet strong -
just like water.

Deep looks in the eyes –
sensual kiss -
and -
our heartbeats sync as we sink into each other.

Finding peace in the moment
is a new favorite thing of mine.
It makes me feel more alive than anything else.
Calm, steady –
only my breathing and my heartbeat remind me
of the physical shell I chose this time.
Everything else floats and hovers around me
and I can feel the energy flowing.

The sacred energy exchange of two souls
and their bodies embracing
and fusing into each other…
Moving slowly, syncing into the same rhythm –
juices flowing, shared kisses...
everything corresponds -
till the energy overflows into pure satisfaction.

I stopped believing in soul-mates -
when I lost what I thought was mine.
And then –
I met you.
And you proved me wrong.
Oh how wrong you proved me.

Wind –
my fellow friend.
Whispering the secrets
of the entire world into my ear.
Not leaving out a single thing –
making sure I hear it all.
So I can carry the legacy in me
until the day it's birthed in the form
of one of my poems, a visual …
or gets lost in the depths
of the chaos of my mind.

Honoring my curves, my unevenness,
my scars, my lines -
my body everyday.

And reminding myself to be good to it,
since it's the shelter - the home of my being.

Women!

Channel your inner Queen!
Recognize other Queens and lift each other up.
Everyone of us has space to glow.

Entirely devoted to myself, my dreams,
my plans, my happiness.
Surrounding myself with the best energies I can find.
Growing, expanding and willingly learning,
to be the best version of myself.

The lines of my body -
Curvy -
Shaping a full, round warmth under these sheets -
reminding you of the sun.

Women.
Different shapes, feels and traits.
Just like the color ways of flowers -
unique in every way.

I'm feeling like a Goddess today.
Appreciating my curves.
Embracing my flaws.
Honoring my womanhood.
I'm feeling like a Goddess today.

Like honey -
the juice of lust is dripping off my leg.
After running down in curves on my inner thigh
as your lips exit the warmth between my legs.

When you suck my lip – tightly.
When you grope my thigh – slightly.
My heart is racing, my head is spinning.
And it feels so right – oh soo right.

Until nothing is felt anymore but us.
Us – merging into each other –
mentally and physically.

Love is a complicated thing.
If you expect too much from one another
without communicating.
But if you speak up and talk it through,
elaborate and are open for compromises
it is the most beautiful,
life changing experience you'll ever have.
Wether it's in a relationship or loving yourself.

I can't stop smiling.

- **D.**

I'm a woman.
Because of all the women in my life:
I'm a strong woman.
I'm a loving woman.
I'm a sexy woman.
I'm a loyal woman.
I'm a hard working woman.
I'm a self confident woman -
And I'm proud to be a woman.

I'm feeling safe, heard, seen and loved
- oh so loved by you.
Your dedication towards the concept of us
being a balanced, happy, steady growing couple
is one of the most beautiful gifts
I ever received.

Your head next to mine –
touching gently.
I hear your heartbeat.

„You smell like summer"
- she said.
He smiled.

You make me smile a thousand times a day –
just by being you.

And when you lay here so peacefully,
I remind myself of how lucky I am to be alive
as this person I chose for this lifetime,
at the same time as you chose yours.
And I know it's meant to be.

It's meant to be that our souls reconnected
in this lifetime and help each other grow.

My chest rises and lowers.
Steady.
Slowly utilizing the space
for the fresh air to expand fully.
I feel everything -

My body, my mind, my soul,
the blood rushing through my veins.
And this -
Balance.

My fingertips are tingling.
A strong energy hovering over my body.
Caressing every inch of my skin gently,
cautious -
yet very present and determined.
I feel peace.

Highly vibrant.
Clearly balanced.
Strongly grateful.
And purely me.

And here it ends.

The last three years of my life, in the most vulnerable,
honest way.
I cried, smiled, loved, and everything in between
while writing these poems and fragments of my
mental and emotional world.
Please hold them lightly.

Thank you for coming on this journey with me.
I appreciate you.

Love and light to you.

THANK YOU

I want to thank everyone that encouraged me and helped me creating my first book.

Thank you to everyone I was able to work with as a creative, especially as a photographer.
I turned some of the pictures I took into illustrations and placed them throughout in this book,
to emphasize the words I used. Having you as a part of this, means a lot to me.
Thank you to Dorjan for encouraging me and leading me into certain, significant directions in life.
Thank you to Hilda, for giving me the last nudge I needed to get to this project.
Thank you to Arletis, Melina, Nadya and Vanessa for editing my final draft. You helped me to be even more precise in what I wanted to express.
Thank you to my family, especially my two mums - Diana and Senka - who always encourage me in my new ideas and life-paths. And lastly, thank you to my old self, for finding a way to express the feelings which led to this journey.